Every Senior

An Educational Experience
Presented by
Dalva Evette Yarrington
Information and Data Scientist

Every School

HIGH SCHOOL

AMERICAN

HISTORY

The Keepsake
Self-Awareness Take-Home

HIGH SCHOOL American HISTORY
The Keepsake Self-Awareness Take-Home
© 2018 Dalva Evette Yarrington

Presenter | Author
Human Development Experience Designer
Information and Data Scientist

ISBN: 1721093125

DEDICATED
To Humanity... you sparkle in your details.

PREFACE

You are on the path to becoming a grown-up. This is a take-home and the data is personal. This academic learning experience is for everyone entering 12th Grade.

The High School American History Take-Home workbook is designed to prepare you for a thorough exploration of American History with you included. You will use digital portals of the National Archives, U. S. Census Population Data, Library-Accessed Websites and explore household paper documents from previous Centuries.

- You should understand that self-awareness is essential to becoming your best self.

- New information requires time to settle into your psyche and resistance reminds you to check your sources and be an honest information broker.

- A historical account should always be at least as accurate as you discovered it and your sources should be cited. Your "Aunt Viv" gets credit for telling you what your mother forgot to tell you or you didn't know to ask.

- When interviewing Elders be respectful and record with permission only! When the memory reservoirs of an Elder are opened they do not close because you have to leave or end the conversation. Provide a means for them to land in a safe place mentally. They know a lot more than you've asked.

- The Elders are a powerful treasure whether you have recognized that fact or not! Happy and safe discoveries await, because you are well-mapped by this workbook.

- **Review the Index before you start. The Experience Index is on page 135.**

- **The best approach is to complete the middle section of each page first and then focus on your Paternal and Maternal Families.**

- **The specifics of this workbook do not have to be shared with your school, teachers or classmates. The experience impact and the research challenges are up for discussion.**

My Maternal Family
My Mother

The Humanity Tour
of

Start Date

My Paternal Family
My Father

My Thoughts About My Maternal Family History

Family History is important to me because...

My Thoughts About My Paternal Family History

My Mother's Birth

Time of Birth

DOB

Place of Birth

Delivered by

Birth Weight

Childhood Health Condition(s)

POD

DOD

Her Father

Her Mother

About My Birth

DOB   Time of Birth

Place of My Birth   My Birth Weight

Delivered by

My Childhood Health Condition(s)

My Father's Birth

Time of Birth

DOB

Place of Birth

Delivered by

Birth Weight

Childhood Health Condition(s)

POD

DOD

His Father

His Mother

More About My Mother's Birth

More About My Birth

More About My Father's Birth

Sources

My Mother's Childhood

She Grew Up With

Her Maternal Birth Order

Her Paternal Birth Order

Her Primary Caregiver(s)/Nurturer(s)

My Mother Was Disciplined by

Places She Grew Up

My Childhood

I Grew Up With

My Maternal Birth Order

My Paternal Birth Order

My Caregivers

Places I Grew Up

My Father's Childhood

He Grew Up With

His Maternal Birth Order

His Paternal Birth Order

His Primary Caregiver(s)/Nurturer(s)

My Father Was Disciplined by

Places He Grew Up

More About My Mother's Childhood Household

About My Childhood Household

Sources

More About My Father's Childhood Household

From - To

Schools My Mother Attended

Schools I Attended	From - To

From - To

Schools My Father Attended

More About My Mother's Education

More About My Education

Sources

More About My Father's Education

My Mother's Occupations and Employers

My Occupations and Employers

My Father's Occupations and Employers

More About My Mother's Toils

More About My Work Life

Sources

More About My Father's Toils

My Mother's Achievements   Timeline

My Achievements   Timeline

My Father's Achievements   Timeline

My Mother's Memberships

My Memberships

My Father's Memberships

Sources

The next pages may contain space for data that does not yet apply to you--
but someday it might. Simply skip through the part of your life that you
have not yet lived. This is a keepsake tool and someday you are likely to
have information for those blanks. Keep filling in your blanks as far as they
apply. Go back and reflect on what you have just learned or been reminded
of.

Now schedule a time to interview each parent or relative so that you can fill
in some of your blanks about your Mother and Father and their families.
Maternal Family is your Mother's family and Paternal Family is your Father's
family.   **The convenience and signature design of this workbook is that the
user can compare and contrast the life of each parent with their own and
thus learn a great deal about history, time, heritage and choices.** A good
solid set of facts about one's own life is key to making decisions, exploring
dreams and taking in new information. Self-knowledge is pivotal. Getting
the facts puts you in a better position to reconcile history and build a good
life for yourself.

There is a space in the back to list words and nomenclature that are new to
your vocabulary and required you to get a working definition.

The Experience Continues

My Mother's Children | DOB

My Children | DOB

My Father's Children | DOB

More About My Mother's Children

More About My Children

More About My Father's Children

Sources

My Mother's Spouses
and Childbearing Mates

My Spouses and Childbearing Mates

My Father's Spouses
and Childbearing Mates

More About My Mother's Mating

About My Mating

Sources

More About My Father's Mating

My Grandchildren

More About My Mother's Grandchildren

More About My Grandchildren

More About My Father's Grandchildren

Sources

My Mother's Grandparents

Paternal Grandfather

Paternal Grandmother

Maternal Grandfather

Maternal Grandmother

My Grandparents

Paternal
Grandfather

Paternal
Grandmother

Maternal
Grandfather

Maternal
Grandmother

My Father's Grandparents

Paternal Grandfather

Paternal Grandmother

Maternal Grandfather

Maternal Grandmother

Nicknames are important and Maiden Names are essential because they are Birth names.

More About My Maternal Great Grandparents

More About My Grandparents

More About My Paternal Great Grandparents

Sources

Foreign Lands of
My Mother's Family

Name	Place or Region

I was born in

At the time of My Birth my Country was led by

News of the Day I was born...

Foreign Lands of
My Father's Family

Name	Place or Region

More About My Maternal Family Origins

More About My Place of Nativity

Population

Form of Governance

Peace, War, Famine etc...

Sources

More About My Paternal Family Origins

Foreign Languages of My Mother's Family

Name	Language or Dialect

Languages Spoken in My Home

Foreign Languages of My Father's Family

Name	Language or Dialect

About My Maternal Family

Languages I Speak

Sources

About My Paternal Family

Religious Traditions of My Mother's Family

Name	Religion

Religious Traditions in My Home

____

____

____

____

____

Religious Traditions of My Father's Family

Name	Religion

More About Maternal Religious Traditions

About My Religious Rites-of-Passage

Sources

More About Paternal Religious Traditions

Ethnic Mixes in My Maternal Family

Name	Ethnicities

Ethnicities in My Home

____

____

____

____

Ethnic Mixes in My Paternal Family

Name	Ethnicities

More About Ethnicity In My Maternal Family

More About Ethnicity and Culture In My Home

Sources

More About Ethnicity In My Paternal Family

About the Tools to Use

THE UNITED STATES CENSUS

This is a key source and should be used in its original form as a matter of course. Find your ancestors in each census taken during their lifetime. Take care to look at the neighbors as you will stumble upon absolutely fascinating details. That is a promise.

Be sure to read the tips and finding-aids of any online database. Archives go to great lengths to have you as informed as possible before granting you access to census records and other documents. Keep in mind that location boundaries have changed over time as well as the names of places. Be sure to research across state, county and municipal boundary lines in census data. A map of the region for the time of a specific census can save you great amounts of time, especially when an index for an enumeration is not available.

Be aware of spelling variations. One example: The midwife who delivered me Lucy [ ] Teate delivered over 350 babies in her career. She married a Louis Teate in Louisiana. If his Mississippi (Tate) family were looking for him in Louisiana, they would need to follow "see" references noted in some digital records pointing to the surname Teate. In the U. S. Census data I found the reuse of first names between the Tate and Teate families striking.

There are also just plain misspellings in both the official U.S. Census enumeration records and in the online transcriptions. One example is: My paternal family name was misspelled as "Yamington" in the 1880 U. S. Census transcription contained in the Familysearch.Org online database of the Church of Jesus Christ of Latter Day Saints. To find my paternal family in their 1880 census transcription, I had to know that in 1880 Great Grandma Anna Hays Yarrington was still living with her mother, my Great, Great Grandmother Ann Bland and where they were living. Ann Bland's name was spelled correctly. I had previously searched her name to find them in the microfilm files in 1985 at the Dallas Public Library. The same cautions about errors apply to other databases.

The great migration from the plantation to the plant influenced family clusters and in my estimation as dramatically as slavery had in the centuries before.

FAMILY MEMBERS WHO KEPT/KEEP RECORDS: ORAL AND OTHERWISE

The first rule here is to ask to take a digital picture of the information written in family Bibles, daybooks and ledgers. Ask to have the family photo albums digitally preserved. Make no mistake -information has great value. Be wary and insure against theft of your information, including paper and digital documents. If the de-facto family archivist refuses to allow you to digitize the collection of treasured family pictures, the best thing is to respect that refusal. The keeper probably knows the value and disrespecting their unwillingness to expose the family treasure will not serve you well later. It is important to make "the ask" clear, as a change of heart may occur. Tell your family member that you would like to do so, and wait until they consent or leave it as inheritance to someone who may be more willing to consent, or who will digitize it themselves and share a copy with you. Respect and diplomacy are paramount within and between family branches.

Many diaries and journals are in trunks and ship-a-robes and some contain jaw-dropping information. You might need a few good nights of sleep after some revelations.

Farmers often maintained detailed crop and transaction records, and sometimes meticulously because of mistrust of the local record-keepers. My maternal grandmother, Alberta (Babe) Meadows Jones kept a household and family event journal. The dollar amount for cotton income and cotton and soybean crop output information is listed by date as well as events such as graduations, baptisms and births. If she had kept a journal during the flood of 1927, it would have been the source for another book. Most of that history was passed down orally. In Hoover's flood she walked for miles and miles carrying my aunt (age four at the time) to higher ground from Newlight to Gilbert, Louisiana slogging through the alligator clay. The most important thing for me is that her journal accounts are is in her own handwriting and my children, grandchildren and nieces will be able to see it and read it. Her journal also gave great insight into what she considered to be important, mentionable and keepsake information. I learned my first archival skills from my maternal grandparents. They used albums and lodge records to instruct me.

SLAVERY

Slavery was an enterprise and there are many ways to search for insights into slave breeding, cotton planting, harvesting and human trafficking.

1860 SLAVEHOLDER CENSUS
 In 2004 when I created the first edition of my genealogy tools, published information giving the names of slaveholders and numbers of slaves held was almost non-existent. That has improved a bit.

> *It is possible to locate an ancestor on a U.S. Census for 1860 or earlier and not know that ancestor was also listed as a slaveholder on the slave schedules, because published indexes almost always do not include the slave census or a "see" reference to the Slaveholder Census. The last U.S. Census Slave Schedules were enumerated by County in 1860 and included 393,975 named persons holding 3,950,546 unnamed slaves, or an average of about ten slaves per holder. [ ] The names of those listed are slaveholders were some of the largest slaveholders in the listed County in 1860.*

Keep in mind that the same systems which impacted Blacks-- also impacted Caucasians, Native Tribal groups and other somewhat distinct ethnic clusters. The outcomes were unique, but none-the-less impactful and breeding a common historic footprint. Sorting through these historic population patterns revealed that, we (humans all of one race) are often reluctant and slow learners from lessons illuminated in inspired texts and letters from thousands of years before. We keep hurting our COUSINS.

ADDITIONAL RESOURCES ON HUMAN SLAVERY MAY BE ACCESSED BY CONSULTING YOUR LOCAL LIBRARY PROFESSIONALS.

FAMILYSEARCH.ORG

This database has existed online in some version or another for some time. I have found it to be a most important change-agent in family history research and in access to genealogical data.

The Family Search database available online for some time was a transcription of the 1880 U.S. Census data and other records. Read the source notes and disclaimers. Use the search tips provided. You will also be able to click to a commercial link for a copy of actual census enumeration pages. I recommend that you get copies of important documentation, but I also recommend that you determine a satisfactory cost-benefit-ratio. The U. S. Census Data underpins what you find here. Some corresponding Canadian enumerations and some Social Security records are also searchable in the Familysearch.Org database.

There are information sharks-- waiting for you in the genealogy enterprise sector.

MARRIAGE BOOKS

Marriage books are a boon for many genealogists-- when they are made available.

From the transcribed and online marriage books in Tensas Parish, Louisiana, I was able to see that Richard (Dick) Jones [born a slave in Edwards, Mississippi] married Ora Bell [daughter of his Louisiana slaveholder and Justice-of-the-Peace] on January 1, 1869. I was also able to see that a person whose family became treasured cousins by marriage later, had stood-up at their wedding. By referencing the 1870 U. S. Census I could also link that person to another side of my family. In fact there was a Bass-Jones connection, a Bass-Meadows connection by labor and that same individual's descendants are connected today on all four sides of my family history.

My family reports Grandpa Dick was "A Tar-Black". Grandma Ora was the mulatto child of the mulatto slave Margaret Walters and the Caucasian plantation owner and Justice of the Peace William Bell of Tensas Parish. William Bell "purchased" Grandpa Dick when he was about 17 and before slavery ended from Dr. William S. Jones in Edwards, Mississippi. That was known from family oral history. Likely, from that same clan of Jones' that later populated the teaching community in the Mississippi River Delta. Grandpa Dick was determined that every one of his offspring knew that he (we) had people in Edwards, Mississippi. That is what it is reported that his mother told him to remember when he was sold away from her. No-doubt his maternal/paternal separation at age 17 caused all great anguish. That one marriage book excursion converging with family oral history brought to light a watershed of additional details. As a follow-up we asked questions of Aunt Alma Jones Bellows, the last living Jones to be rocked on the lap of that former slave.

The digital transcribers of marriage books and other county records have often been volunteers from local historical societies or social groups. You will find some errors, but much of the work is outstanding.

In the case of the books referenced above, Edith Ziegler was the able and generous transcriber. When you come across such generous work it is more than appropriate to send a thank you note whenever possible and always acknowledge transcribers in your narratives and compilations. Mind-you, some data collection and transcriptions are corrupted by oil and mineral greed and others by poorly informed transcribers. Original records are always preferable.
Many of these records are now scanned and that is significant as it removes or reduces the likelihood of secondary transcription errors.

NATIONAL ARCHIVES AND RECORDS ADMINISTRATION (NARA)

According to its website, NARA holds in trust over 5 billion pages of textual records; more than 14 million still pictures; about 300,000 reels of motion picture film; over 200,000 sound recordings; more than 15 million maps, charts, and aerial photographs; and over 170,000 electronic records files. The collections of NARA document the point where the lives of private citizens have intersected with the functions of the federal government. Census records, passenger lists, military service records, and land records can be found in the National Archives. The NARA website should be carefully consulted for further information on the scope of collections and on access. The National Archive and Records Administration "copies of records" can also be cost prohibitive for many. Cost comparison is appropriate. A trip to a regional branch of NARA can be useful when planned well. Having been the student of a former National Archivist (Dean Warner) I hold that standards were established and are hopefully currently being maintained.

BIRTH RECORDS

Birth records are collected at the county level and usually filed in duplicate at the state level. Many changes and upgrades have occurred in vital records management. Some were actually sound changes. Some states have very questionable standards in records management and access.   In the aftermath of Hurricane Katrina many documents and vital paper records were at risk of loss.

You will need to check with the local county clerk for perhaps the best approach to a records search. Local civil servant archivists should share their wealth of tips with you when you request a consultative appointment. Experienced genealogist can be extraordinarily helpful in record and search queries for a price.

CHURCH RECORDS

Churches have always been a primary source for community records of various types. Check with the church personally to view, copy down or even be allowed to make a digital copy of event and circumstance information.

Never ask and never take Church or institutional documents out of the care of the custodian. Old documents should be handled with care and a fresh set of virgin cotton gloves is always appropriate, when allowed to handle important materials. Rare bookroom rules should be the norm when viewing one-of-a-kind, original and old treasured documents and artifacts.

DEATH RECORDS/ OBITUARIES

News reporting organizations (newspapers) are a rich source of reported deaths and events. They know that the information could be priceless, so ask up-front about fees and fashion your strategy accordingly. Even when cost is no object you should be careful of information access extortionist. Going to the library to search the newspapers on microfilm or fiche is likely cheaper. An obituary is often a family tree abstract and can offer clues on places lived, people married and work done as well as religious affiliations.

County governments are custodians of birth, death and tax data among other local government data sets. Be aware of fees and not afraid to question appropriateness of excesses.

My Family in
U. S. Census Records
and in Other Census Records

Maternal Family Members Found In the 1940 U. S. Census

Name	County/State/Age/Page

My Research in the 1940 Census

____

____

____

____

____

Paternal Family Members Found In the 1940 U. S. Census

Name	County/State/Age/Page

More About Maternal Family
in the 1940 U. S. Census

More About What I Found in the 1940 U. S. Census

More About Paternal Family
in the 1940 U. S. Census

Maternal Family Members Found In the 1930 U. S. Census

Name	County/State/Age/Page

My Research in the 1930 Census

____

____

____

____

____

Paternal Family Members Found In the 1930 U. S. Census

Name	County/State/Age/Page

More About Maternal Family
in the 1930 U. S. Census

More About What I Found in the 1930 U. S. Census

More About Paternal Family
in the 1930 U. S. Census

Maternal Family Members Found In the 1920 U. S. Census

Name	County/State/Age/Page

My Research in the 1920 Census

____

____

____

____

Paternal Family Members Found In the 1920 U. S. Census

Name	County/State/Age/Page

More About Maternal Family
in the 1920 U. S. Census

More About What I Found in the 1920 U. S. Census

More About Paternal Family
in the 1920 U. S. Census

Maternal Family Members Found
In the 1910 or 1900 U. S. Census

Name	County/State/Age/Page

My Research in the 1910 or 1900 U. S. Census

____

____

____

____

Paternal Family Members Found
In the 1910 or 1900 U. S. Census

Name	County/State/Age/Page

More About Maternal Family
in the 1910 or 1900 U. S. Census

More About What I Found in the 1910 or 1900 U. S. Census

More About Paternal Family
in the 1910 or 1900 U. S. Census

Maternal Family Members Found In the 1880 U. S. Census

Name	County/State/Age/Page

My Research in the 1880 U. S. Census

___

___

___

___

___

Paternal Family Members Found In the 1880 U. S. Census

Name	County/State/Age/Page

More About Maternal Family
in the 1880 U. S. Census

More About What I Found in the 1880 U. S. Census

More About Paternal Family
in the 1880 U. S. Census

Maternal Family Members Found
In the 1870 or 1860 U. S. Census

Name	County/State/Age/Page

My Research in the1870 or 1860   U. S. Census

Paternal Family Members Found
In the 1870 or 1860 U. S. Census

Name	County/State/Age/Page

More About Maternal Family
in the 1870 or 1860 U. S. Census

More About What I Found in the 1870 or 1860 U. S. Census

More About Paternal Family
in the 1870 or 1860 U. S. Census

Maternal Family Members Found in Other U. S. Census

Name	County/State/Age/Page

My Research in Other U.S. Census Records

____

____

____

____

Paternal Family Members Found in Other U. S. Census

Name	County/State/Age/Page

More About What I Found in the Other U. S. Census Records

Maternal Family Members Found in Other Census Collections

Name	Describe and Cite

My Research in Other Census Collections

Paternal Family Members Found in Other Census Collections

Name	Describe and Cite

More About What I Found in Other Census Collections

More About Maternal Family
in Other Census Collections

More About Paternal Family
in Other Census Collections

People who kept and shared
Maternal History

Family History and Albums in My Home

Sources

People who kept and shared
Paternal History

About Maternal Documents and Records

Family Documents I Keep

About Paternal Documents and Records

Sources

Maternal Oral Historians

Family Stories I Have Shared

Paternal Oral Historians

Sources

More About Maternal Family Lore

More Family Lore

Sources

More About Paternal Family Lore

Maternal Family Connections To Fame

Name	Famous Connection

My Connection(s) To Fame

____

____

____

____

Sources

Paternal Family Connections To Fame

Name	Famous Connection

More About Maternal Fame and Infamy

About Fame and Infamy

Sources

More About Paternal Fame and Infamy

Maternal Connections to
Original Land Grants

Name	Location

About My Connections to Land

____

____

____

____

____

Sources

Paternal Connections to
Original Land Grants

Name	Location

Inherited Original Land Grant Assets

Sources

Maternal Native or Indigenous Americans

Name	Tribe/Group...

My Known Native American Connection(s)

Paternal Native or Indigenous Americans

Name	Tribe/Group...

Sources

Dominant Maternal Cultural Identities

My Dominant Cultural Identity

Dominant Paternal Cultural Identities

My Maternal Grandmother's
Brothers and Sisters

My Mother's Aunts

My Mother's Uncles

My Maternal Grandmother had a Total of # _______ Children

My Maternal Grandfather Had a Total of # _______ Children

My Maternal Grandfather's
Brothers and Sisters

My Mother's Aunts

My Mother's Uncles

Sources

Sources

My Paternal Grandmother's
Brothers and Sisters

My Father's Aunts

My Father's Uncles

My Paternal Grandmother had a Total of #_______ Children

My Paternal Grandfather Had a Total of #_______ Children

My Paternal Grandfather's
Brothers and Sisters

My Father's Aunts

My Father's Uncles

Wealthy Maternal Family Members

Name	Description

Wealth in My Home

____

____

____

____

____

Wealthy Paternal Family Members

Name	Description

Sources

Sources

More About Maternal Wealth

About Generational Family Wealth

More About Paternal Wealth

Maternal Sharecroppers

Name	Location

My Cooperative Experiences

____

____

____

____

____

Paternal Sharecroppers

Name	Location

Sources

More About Maternal Agricultural Economics

Economic Disparities of My Lifetime

More About Paternal Agricultural Economics

Maternal Family Shopkeepers

Name	Location / Type

My Shopkeeping, Sales and Marketing Experiences

____

____

____

____

Paternal Family Shopkeepers

Name	Location / Type

Sources

More About Maternal Shopkeeping

More

More About Paternal Shopkeeping

Maternal Family Hoteliers and Innkeepers

Name	Location

Landlords. Innkeepers etc.

____

____

____

____

____

Sources

Paternal Family Hoteliers and Innkeepers

Name	Location

More About Maternal Landlords. Innkeepers etc.

More

Sources

More About Paternal Landlords. Innkeepers etc.

Sources

Maternal Farmers, Ranchers and Grocers

Name	Location							

My Connection to Farming, Ranching and Grocery Chains

____

____

____

____

____

Maternal Farmers, Ranchers and Grocers

Name	Location							

Sources

More About Agricultural Food
and Maternal Family Members

More about Agricultural Food and Me

More About Agricultural Food
and Paternal Family Members

Sources

Maternal Manufacturers, Designers and Crafters

Product	Name

Things I Make, Design or Craft

____

____

____

____

____

Paternal Manufacturers, Designers and Crafters

Product	Name

More About Products I Make, Design or Craft

Sources

Maternal Family Visual Artist and Art Dealers

Name	Describe

My Relationship with Visual Arts

____

____

____

____

Paternal Family Visual Artist and Art Dealers

Name	Describe

Sources

Sources

About My Maternal Family in the Arts Industry

More

About My Paternal Family in the Arts Industry

Maternal Family Elected and Appointed Officials

Name	Office/Location

My Elected and Appointed Positions

____

____

____

____

____

Paternal Family Elected and Appointed Officials

Name	Office/Location

Sources

More About My Maternal Family Officeholders

More about My Community, Stare and National Positions

Sources

More About My Paternal Family Officeholders

Maternal Family Military Service

Name	Branch/War/Dates

My Military Service

____

____

____

____

____

Paternal Family Military Service

Name	Branch/War/Dates

Sources

More About Maternal Military Service

More About My Service

More About Paternal Military Service

Sources

Maternal Family Preachers and Clergy

Name	Denomination and Location

My Relationship with Preaching and Religious Teaching

____

____

____

____

Paternal Family Preachers and Clergy

Name	Denomination and Location

Sources

More About Maternal Family Clergy

More About My Religious Calling and Training

Sources

More About Paternal Family Clergy

Maternal Family Tax Collectors and Undertakers

Name	Describe/Location

My Relationship With Tax Collecting and Undertaking

____

____

____

____

Paternal Family Tax Collectors and Undertakers

Name	Describe/Location

Sources

More About Tax Collecting and Undertaking

Sources

More About Maternal Family
Tax Collectors and Morticians

More About Paternal Family
Tax Collectors and Morticians

Maternal Family Bootleggers and etc.

Name	Product/Location

My Relationship with Home-Brewing

____

____

____

____

Paternal Family Bootleggers and etc.

Name	Product/Location

Sources

More About Maternal Family
Unlawful Enterprises

More Speaking Easy

More About Paternal Family
Unlawful Enterprises

Incarcerated Maternal Family Members

Name	Crime/ Location

My Relationship with Incarceration

____

____

____

____

Sources

Incarcerated Paternal Family Members

Name	Language or Dialect

More About Incarceration

Maternal Family Doctors, Nurses and Midwives

Name	Specialty/Location

My Relationship with Health Practitioners

____

____

____

____

____

Paternal Family Doctors, Nurses and Midwives

Name	Specialty/Location

Sources

Sources

More About Maternal Family Health Practitioners

More About Health Care Practitioners in My Life

More About Paternal Family Health Practitioners

Sources

Maternal Family Teachers, Authors Professors and Researchers

Name	Subject/Location

My Relationship with Teaching, Research and Education

____

____

____

____

Paternal Family Teachers, Authors Professors and Researchers

Name	Subject/Location

More About Teachers and Education in My Life

Maternal Family Engineers and Scientist

Name	Discipline/Industry

My Relationship with Engineering and Science

____

____

____

____

____

Sources

Paternal Family Engineers and Scientist

Name	Discipline/Industry

More About Maternal Family
Engineers and Scientist

More About Engineers and Scientist in My Life

Sources

More About Paternal Family
Engineers and Scientist

Sources

Maternal Family Cooks, Chefs and Bakers

Name	Areas of Expertise

My Food Skills

____

____

____

____

Paternal Family Cooks, Chefs and Bakers

Name	Areas of Expertise

More About Maternal Family Food Cuisine

More About My Food Skills

Sources

More About Paternal Family Food Cuisine

Maternal Family Construction Industry Workers

Name	Skill/Industry Area

My Relationship with Construction

____

____

____

____

Paternal Family Construction Industry Workers

Name	Skill/Industry Area

Sources

Sources

More About Maternal Family
Skilled Trade Workers

My Construction Skills

More About Paternal Family
Skilled Trade Workers

Maternal Family in Automotives and Mechanics

Name	Describe

My Relationship with Automobiles and Mechanics

____

____

____

____

____

Paternal Family in Automotives and Mechanics

Name	Describe

Sources

Sources

More About Maternal Family Auto Makers, Dealers and Mechanics

More About Automobiles and My Life

More About Paternal Family Auto Makers, Dealers and Mechanics

Sources

Maternal Family Bankers, Stock Traders and Insurance Agents

Name	Specify/Location

My Relationship with Bankers, Traders and Agents

____

____

____

____

Paternal Family Bankers, Stock Traders and Insurance Agents

Name	Specify/Location

More About Maternal Family Money Traders

More about the Financial Industry and My Life

Sources

More About Paternal Family Money Traders

Sources

Maternal Family Musical Artist or Managers

Name	Describe

My Relationship with the Music Industry

____

____

____

____

____

Paternal Family Musical Artist or Managers

Name	Describe

About My Maternal Family in the Music Industry

More

Sources

About My Paternal Family in the Music Industry

Maternal Family Athletes

Name	Sport/Team/Records

My Relationship with Sports and Athletics

____

____

____

____

____

Paternal Family Athletes

Name	Sport/Team/Records

Sources

More About Maternal Family Athletics

More about My Sports and Recreation

Sources

More About Paternal Family Athletics

Maternal Family Seamstresses, Tailors and Cobblers

Name	Specify/Describe

My Relationship with Sewing and Clothing Construction

____

____

____

____

Sources

Paternal Family Seamstresses, Tailors and Cobblers

Name	Specify/Describe

More About Maternal Family Clothing
and Shoe Makers

More About My Clothing and Shoemaking

Sources

More About Paternal Family Clothing
and Shoe Makers

Maternal Family Logistics, Postal and Delivery Workers

Name	Service/Firm/Location

My Relationship with Logistics Work

____

____

____

____

____

Sources

Paternal Family Logistics, Postal and Delivery Workers

Name	Service/Firm/Location

More About Maternal Family
Distribution Workers

More About Logistics Workers

Sources

More About Paternal
Distribution Workers

Maternal Family Members Who Were Physically or Mentally Disadvantaged or Injured

Name	Describe

My Physical and Mental Challenges

Sources

Paternal Family Members Who Were Physically or Mentally Disadvantaged or Injured

Name	Describe

More About Maternal Disabilities

Physical and Mental Challenges I Have Overcome

Sources

More About Paternal Disabilities

Maternal Family Members Who Were Abandoned

Name	Age/Location

My Relationship with Abandonment

____

____

____

____

____

Sources

Paternal Family Members Who Were Abandoned

Name	Age/Location

Sources

More About Maternal Abandonment and Orphans

More About Abandonment

More About Paternal Abandonment and Orphans

Maternal Family Members Who Were Murdered

Name	Explained

My Relationship with Murder

____

____

____

____

Sources

Paternal Family Members Who Were Murdered

Name	Explained

Sources

More About Murdered
Maternal Family Members

More About Murder and Tragedy

More About Murdered
Paternal Family Members

Sources

Maternal Family Members Found in Marriage Books

Name	County/State/Year/Page

My Marriage Dates

____

____

____

____

Paternal Family Members Found in Marriage Books

Name	County/State/Year/Page

More About My Marriages

Sources

Maternal Family Found in Immigration Records

Name	Port/State/Year/Page

My Immigration History

____

____

____

____

____

Paternal Family Found in Immigration Records

Name	Port/State/Year/Page

More About My Citizenship

Maternal Family Members Found in Slave Records

Name	County/State/Year/Page

My Relationship with Enslavement

____

____

____

____

Paternal Family Members Found in Slave Records

Name	County/State/Year/Page

Sources

More About Maternal Enslavement

More About My Slavery Heritage

Sources

More About Paternal Enslavement

Sources

Maternal Family Members Found In State Historical Collections

Name	Keyword/State/Year/Page

States I Have Made History In

____

____

____

____

Paternal Family Members Found In State Historical Collections

Name	Keyword/State/Year/Page

More About Maternal Family
in State Historical Collections

More About Me in State Collections

Sources

More About Paternal Family
in State Historical Collections

Sources

Maternal Family Members Found in The National Archives (NARA) or Smithsonian Collections

Name	Collection/Link/Room

My Relationship with NARA and The Smithsonian

____

____

____

____

Paternal Family Members Found in The National Archives (NARA) or Smithsonian Collections

Name	Collection/Link/Room

Sources

More About Maternal Family
in National Collections

More About National Records and My Life

More About Paternal Family
in National Collections

Sources

Maternal Family Members Found on National Memorial Walls, Monuments and Statuary

Name	Describe/Location

My Relationship With National Monuments and Walls

Paternal Family Members Found on National Memorial Walls, Monuments and Statuary

Name	Describe/Location

Sources

More About Maternal Family on Monuments and Recognition Sites

More About Me, Monuments and Recognition Sites

More About Paternal Family on Monuments and Recognition Sites

Sources

Maternal Family Members Found In Other Collections

Name	Type/Location

My Relationship with Other Historic Collections or Publications

____

____

____

____

Paternal Family Members Found In Other Collections

Name	Type/Location

More About Maternal Family
in Other Collections

More About Me in Other Historic Collections

Sources

More About Paternal Family
in Other Collections

Maternal Family Members Living the Longest Lives

Name	DOB/DOD

My Current Age

____

____

____

____

Sources

Paternal Family Members Living the Longest Lives

Name	DOB/DOD

More About Maternal Family Longest Lives

My Life Expectancy

Sources

More About Paternal Family Longest Lives

Maternal Family Members Living the Shortest Lives

Name	DOB/DOD/Cause

My Current Health Status

Sources

Paternal Family Members Living the Shortest Lives

Name	DOB/DOD/Cause

My Father's Life Span   -

My Mother's Life Span   -

Common Causes of Maternal Death

Name	Specify

Maternal Sources of Death Information

____

____

____

Paternal Sources of Death Information

____

____

Common Causes of Paternal Death

Sources

Name	Specify

Unusual Causes of Maternal Death

Mysterious Family Deaths

Unusual Causes of Paternal Death

Sources

Maternal Places of Burial

Name	Method/Location

I expect to be buried at ___________________

____

____

____

____

Sources

Paternal Places of Burial

Name	Method/Location

More About Maternal Family
Funerals and Burials

How I want to be Memorialized or Celebrated

Sources

More About Paternal Family
Funerals and Burials

Census of Places My Maternal Family Lived

Name	Location

Census of Places My Paternal Family Lived

Name	Location

Godparents in My Maternal family

Name	God Parent To

My Godparents

I am the Godparent to

Sources

Godparents in My Paternal family

Name	Godparent to

Sources

Extended Maternal Family Members

About My Current Extended Family Members

Extended Paternal Family Members

Maternal Heirloom Recipes

Dish Name		
Ingredients		

Directions

Dish Name		
Ingredients		

Directions

Paternal Heirloom Recipes

Dish Name		
Ingredients		

Directions

Dish Name		
Ingredients		

Directions

More Maternal Family Notes

I.

II.

More Paternal Family Notes

I.

II.

Experience Index
and Tour Outline A-Z

New Words and Phrases

Word or Phrase	Defines or Explaines
	149

For A Lifetime
Keepsake Workbook.

The data you can't find today could very well be located tomorrow.
This is now your reference and you will not be a missing link
in your child's personal history.

One Human Race, Each of Us Ethnically Unique!

This publication intends to support
**2020 Human Development
Goals of the United Nations**

An Educational Publication Distributed through AMAZON.Com

ISBN: 1721093125

$14.99 U.S.D.

Other Important Editions of this Experience

College Level Sociology 101
Psychology 101
Populations Studies 101

College Level Introduction to
Mexican-American Culture and Heritage
Mexican Population Studies
Texas Studies

College and Professioal Startups
Engineering 101
Enterprise 101
Operations and Human Resources
Business Psychology
Markets and People

Self-Awareness is a Fundamental Human Rite-of-Passage